A WILD ADVENTURE

Fragments from the Life of

THOMAS WATLING
DUMFRIES CONVICT ARTIST

TOM POW

For Julie

First published in Great Britain in 2014 by Polygon, an imprint of Birlinn Ltd,
West Newington House, 10 Newington Road, Edinburgh EH9 1QS
www.polygonbooks.co.uk

ISBN: 978 1 84697 287 4
British Library Cataloguing-in-Publication Data
A catalogue record for this book is available on request from the British Library.

Design by Teresa Monachino.
Printed and bound in Slovenia.

A WILD ADVENTURE:

CONTENTS

A WILD ADVENTURE:
ILLUSTRATIONS

Also features on the cover.

THOMAS WATLING:
BIOGRAPHICAL
NOTES

Thomas Watling was born in September 1762, the son of Ham Watlin, a soldier; mother unknown. Both of Watling's parents died when he was an infant and he was brought up by his Aunt Marion (a.k.a. May). He showed skill as an artist and started his own academy where he taught "drawing to ladies and gentlemen for a guinea a month".

In 1788, he was arrested and charged with forging twelve one-guinea notes. (A guinea was worth roughly £60 in today's money.) He claimed, lamely, that it was an experiment and he had had no intention of passing the notes off as real. Trial was fixed for 14 April 1789. Forty-five witnesses were lined up against him. Forgery was a capital offence – so serious a crime that, in England, women could still be burnt at the stake for committing it. Watling filed a petition, requesting transportation to save his neck, and was sentenced to fourteen years in the newly founded penal colony of Botany Bay, Australia.

On board the *Peggy*, from Leith to Plymouth, Watling and another prisoner, Paton, foiled an attempted mutiny. In recompense, Paton was pardoned, but Watling was judged "an acquisition to the new Colony at Botany Bay" because of his skills as "an ingenious Artist". And so, Thomas Watling was co-opted as an unwilling player in what Richard Holmes has termed "The Age of Wonder".

In 1788, when the First Fleet had sailed to Botany Bay, fourteen officers on board the ships had publishing contracts. There were two principle reasons for this. The first was that the reports of Captain Cook's First Pacific Voyage, 1768-71, contained tales from Tahiti of sexual freedoms that tantalised eighteenth-century society, and it wanted more of the same. The second reason is that, in the mid-eighteenth century, botany was a science of great interest. Carl Linnaeus's botanic classifications, identifying plants by male and female parts, had sexualised botany to the extent that mixed botanic outings were frowned upon in polite society. In fact, so hot were plants at the time, a book on botany would likely be given with a plain or disguising cover. Previously, specimens of flora and fauna had been sent home by sea for illustrative purposes. Unsurprisingly, many did not survive the passage. What a boon to have someone on the spot who could churn out illustrations for free.

So, in 1791, Watling set sail for Australia on the *Pitt*. He enjoyed a short spell of liberty in the Cape of Good Hope, before being betrayed by "the mercenary Dutch". The Colony at which he eventually arrived in 1792 was a little over four years old; Watling described it as being about one third of the size of Dumfries.

Watling was the first professional artist in the colony – the first artist who wasn't constrained by naval training. He was seconded to Surgeon-General John White, whose *Journal of a Voyage to New South Wales* had already been published in 1790. White kept Watling busy producing illustrations for his next projected book. Watling described White as a "haughty despot" and objected to being "lent about as a household utensil to his neighbours" – further sign of his value as an artist to the colony.

In 1794, Watling's own *Letters from an Exile in Botany Bay to his Aunt in Dumfries* was published in Penrith, a slim chapbook filled with lively descriptions of the richness of Australia's flora and fauna. He is dismissive of the natural inhabitants of New South Wales and defensive of his own position: "Instances of oppression and mean sordid despotism are so glaring and frequent as to banish every hope of generosity and urbanity from such as I am."

As you would expect, his embittered judgement on the colonisers' enterprise is scathing: "The face of the country is deceitful, having every appearance of fertility and yet productive of no one article in itself fit for the support of mankind."

Watling was pardoned in 1797, having served eight years of his fourteen-year sentence, and he left Australia, likely returning to Dumfries via Calcutta, where a Watling was recorded in 1801, 1802 and 1803, working as a miniaturist. There is little doubt that this was Thomas Watling. For one thing, a pardon did not come with a ticket back to England; Watling would have had to earn enough for his passage to Calcutta and then onwards. Ship owners charged £100 for a one-way ticket from Calcutta to London – a huge amount of money and reason why the young East India Company writers, whose wage was £5 per year, had to make a success of their Indian venture if they were ever to see their homeland again.

One explanation for the lack of evidence concerning Watling in Calcutta is that it is likely he would have been living between two worlds – the world of White Town and the world of Black Town. Nor would he have had the unique artistic value he had enjoyed in Port Sydney. There were many artists of note working in India at the time. As a portraitist, Watling would not have access to the front rank of Calcuttan society. And perhaps he never escaped the stigma of being an ex-convict, an undesirable. The *Calcutta Gazette* reported, on 3 July 1800, "By the Most Noble the Governor General in Council. Proclamation. This prohibits the landing of ex-convicts from New South Wales in Bengal and requires any already there to leave by 1st March 1801."

Whether Watling was one of those affected by this order or not, by 1804 he was back in Dumfries, employed as an art master at Dumfries Academy, and supplementing his income by taking commissions painting houses, coaches and signs. *A Direct North General View of Sydney Cove*, 1794, the earliest known oil painting of Australia, may have been painted in Dumfries at this time, though its provenance is disputed. An inscription on the back reads "Painted immediately from nature by T. Watling".

One of the mysteries in Watling's life is his inability to have made something more substantial of himself on his return to Dumfries. After all, by this point he had become a talented artist, accomplished in a range of genres which were very desirable – landscape, nature painting, scientific study, and miniatures. Moreover, he had a story to tell. Of the few who left Scotland's shores for New South Wales (only 4.8% of those transported were Scots) how many had returned? Whether as a result of failings in opportunity or in character or simply through prejudice against his initial crime, in 1806 he was arrested and charged once again with forgery – this time for forging at least seven five-guinea notes. Incredibly, given the evidence linking Watling directly with the forged notes, the jury found the case not proven and he was freed. And then the trail goes cold – until, in an undated letter c. 1814, aged 52 or thereabouts and in ill health, he writes from London to Admiral Hunter, the former Governor of the Colony, asking for financial help.

It is difficult to find much information about Watling – especially in the years prior to his transportation and those upon his return. It is a life, as it has come to us, and perhaps as he himself experienced it, of fragments. Such fragments presented here (in unstable variations of the eighteenth century's ubiquitous couplet) are drawn from historical evidence, supplemented by empathy and imagination.

And in between its greatest obscurities, infinitely more precious than the prejudices of his *Letters*, we have the visual record he left, the Watling Collection, part of the First Fleet Collection, now kept in the Natural History Museum in London. Here, there are paintings of what became "type specimens", as well as a visual record of the Australians who were, in these parts, so close to their eventual oblivion: evidence of what this "genius in bondage" achieved in his time in Australia.

TOM POW
Dumfries, April 2014

For images of Watling's work, go to the Natural History Museum / First Fleet / Watling Collection

A first North view of Sydney Cove and Port Jackson the chief British Settlement in New South Wales. Taken from the North Shore about one mile distant for John White Esqr.

A WILD
ADVENTURE

"To see what has been done in the space of five or six years, of clearing, building and planting, is astonishing. I humbly declare that it is my opinion, that all that has been done is of little service [and a] wild adventure."

THOMAS WATLING, *Letters from an Exile
at Botany Bay to his Aunt in Dumfries*

"I saw *everything*, so the question now is not what I saw, but *how* I saw it."

ANTON CHEKHOV, from a letter to Alexey Suvorin, 11 September 1890, regarding his trip to the penal colony on Sakhalin Island.

"Home is the first
and final poem"

LES MURRAY, *Home Suite*

THE PUBLISHER OF THE ENSUING PRODUCTION,
SENDS IT INTO THE WORLD
FOR THE TWO FOLLOWING REASONS.

...

FIRST; he hopes it may contribute a little to the relief of an old, infirm, and friendless woman, to whom it is addressed.

And SECONDLY; he imagines, the account given here of a country so little known, may be interesting to some, and amusing to ALL. With the original, which is now in his hands, he declines taking any liberty, but leaves the unfortunate exile to tell his story exactly in his own words, and how he acquits himself, the public must determine. The publisher has several letters from the same author still in his hands; and should these meet with a favourable reception, they are intended to be published, together with a life of the author on some future occasion.

The introduction to LETTERS from AN EXILE at BOTANY BAY to his AUNT in DUMFRIES; giving a particular account of the settlement of NEW SOUTH WALES with the Customs and Manners of the INHABITANTS. [Price - six-pence]

PRELUDE: A WORLD OF LIGHT

It's a small attic room and there's light –
The good light he needs – from a lamp

On the table before him. His eyesight's
Not what it was. At times his hand cramps

When he needs it to be steady, as he steers
His pen round the double-cupped curve

That begins *Bank*. Sometimes, he'll squeeze a tear
Of concentration; through it catch the swerve

Of a bird, its plumage smudged in shadows.
He gave them all the pictures they asked for –

The Channel Bill, the Needle-tailed Swallow -
But he should've attended to their calls.

Then the common cries of pigeon and crow
Couldn't confuse him. There wouldn't be a note

Or a song that, from this cold room, could draw
Him back to a world that was carved from light.

PART ONE:
ARREST

*"the most wretched and
unhappy of all mankind"*

THE BANK OF SCOTLAND ADVISES ITS
DUMFRIES AGENT DAVID STAIG, 20 SEPT 1788

Beware of giving the suspect alarm.
Rather indulge his security: smile

As if all but he would wish you harm.
When the warrant is issued, arrive while

He will least expect it. Approach his house
At dawn or in the small hours of the night.

Fear not, he will be trapped as any louse
In candle-flame. We have him in our sights.

But *enjoin silence* to the Gentlemen
Of your office. Let it be moon silence

Or else the feigned silence of the peahen,
Dazed by majesty, yet through the cold lens

Of its black eyes knowing what must be done.
We will match each false cut and curlicue.

Enjoin silence. The Forger's luck has run.
This, Agent Staig, is how we instruct you.

WATLING, CAPTURED, HAS A NEW SENSE OF SELF

And, at that moment, when the door darkened,
And the game was up, then, you must have known

Exactly who you were; felt likened
To the weight of a stone, knowing it's stone

And can be none other. No, not the quill
Of a gull floating downstream. Less the wheep

Of a peewit recalled from the bald hills.
Or the cormorant's crook, the rotting sheep,

The flicker of a candle flame over
A hand that is not your own. None of these.

For, all things that have sent you from yourself
Have returned to yourself. And so, the core

Of Watlinghood, you lean on your scratched desk
And your world turns like a freshly cast key.

Ah, this, perhaps, is how it feels *to be*.
Your thin voice cracks through the cold, "Aye, that's me."

WATLING, IN HIS OWN DEFENCE

Your Honours, my defence: How can an Artist
Improve without challenge? What challenge greater

Than that which should be refused? The gist
Of my argument is there. It is not the bearer

Of the bill, but the Artist, who innocently sees
The wave in its calligraphy; the lifeline's hopes

In its faint print. Often in a drawing of leaves
The same pen will express similar strokes.

Besides, the crime of forgery consists
Not simply in imitation, but rather

In putting such copy to use. I rest
My defence with this conceit: that murder

Involves more than forging the weapon.
You think this weak? May I offer then, with leaden

Heart, my transportation? I'd rather leg it
Than remain where I've no degree of credit.

HIS AUNT MAY SPEAKS UP

Your Honours, my Thomas is a good boy
In his heart. It was I who brought him up.

His father, Ham, was a soldier, but died
Soon after his poor mother. *He* could sup

With the Devil, if you'll pardon me, Sirs.
Thomas is a fair artist as you know

And held in esteem by both boys and girls
At his Drawing School. I am old. The snow

Will be falling soon. What shall I do
With my Thomas away? Who'll tend my hearth?

Sirs, you should know Thomas can appear vain.
Take it no more than a mark of his talent.

It's in his temperament to see through
The empty show to a man's true worth.

He leaves for New Holland with only one stain.
Relent! Let me see my Thomas again.

WATLING'S DIRGE: SCOTIA FAREWELL!

O Scotia, farewell, we leave you behind,
  A Flame to tend in the Dark of our Minds.

We must set Sail for a Land faraway
  With grim Thoughts of how we've ruin'd our Days.

We should've paid Heed to those better than us;
  We pray they'll forgive our Betrayals of Trust.

But Scotia has granted the fallen Hope –
  In Kindness we have been spared the Rope.

Between us soon will lie the World's great Seas –
  Dear God protect us, we're on bended Knees!

On a distant soil we'll cry Tears for Home,
  For the Hills and the Skies where Curlews roam.

With our Tears we'll help this young Land to grow,
  To become rich on the Seeds of Sorrow.

Then our Wretchedness won't have been in Vain
  And Scotia pass under another's Name.

PART TWO:
TRANSPORTATION

"genius in bondage"

ON BOARD SHIP, BOUND FOR THE COLONY

Early days for the moonshots, each voyage
A giant leap for mankind, the *ur*–

Technology threadbare, chancy. Even
So, a rough settlement of sorts awaits,

Improvised in dust. In the reeking hold
Below the fo'c'sle, men are chained in racks –

Besmirched, befouled, be-shat – as the ship
Bucks and rolls; thrusts through darkest capes of space,

Humming a ballad of its own demise.
Watling peers through a slit in molten plates,

Tries to hold in focus, through stinging eyes,
His world spinning from him – a roundel

Of bruised blue and green light, forever now
Beyond his grasp. While ahead lies the faint

Watermark of their *Terra Nullius*,
Foxed with curiously silvered seas.

WATLING, SURPRISED, ON ARRIVAL

It's October 1792.
A man, shielding his eyes, pulls through blue

Sunlit water, the leg irons he bears.
One of many so weighed down, he stares

Past a shabby settlement of crude huts
To the knit of dull shrub beyond. The cuts

In his ankles shiver in the brine. Short
For his age, his clothes are rags and dirt

From the many months he's been at sea.
One half of him knows he'll have to please;

The other turns to his custodians
A pair of brazen, something-coloured eyes.

In such a way the *Survivor* is marked.
He can't show his fear of the coming dark.

Rather, aching with regret, yet alert –
Just there! a small bird, like a crimson dart.

THE FORGER'S FIRST LESSON

Attached to Surgeon-General John White,
The irony isn't lost on Watling

That his first given task on arrival
(Courtesy of the Royal Admiral)

Is to copy with care what lies within
A pencil frame, learning to get it right.

That Brown Grackle, crudely done by another,
Involves paying attention to the colour,

The curve of the head, the way the feathers
Lie, just so, over pale leg markings.

He learns too how the object must be placed;
How a curtailed landscape is in good taste.

Perforce, they'll look afresh at bird and beggar!
When he, in cursive, signs *Thomas Watling,*

His bird will show what can never be taught –
It breathes with life, like a crisp guinea note.

THE AFTERLIFE OF NAMES

Precise in such matters, the Australians
Had use of many names throughout their lives –

And one which died with them. The crime
You committed (twice) means your steadfast pride

Ensures "Thomas Watling" shall live, twice named.
First as forger, a lowly supplicant.

Then, as one who plays a different game,
Who sees his signature as lubricant

To lasting fame; who despises John White,
He who advises, "on publication,

The name [Watling] may be left out". (A blight
On one who'd deny an Artist his station!)

For all that, *T. W.*, you're elusive
For us now . . . I hear your heart race

As you crouch close to earth like a rabbit.
(The poacher passes, boots on frosted grass.)

THE VAST NUMBER of green frogs, reptiles, and large insects, among the grass and on the trees, during the spring, summer, and fall, make an incessant noise and clamour. They cannot fail to surprise the stranger exceedingly, as he will hear their discordant croaking just by, and sometimes all around him, though he is unable to discover whence it proceeds: - nor can he perceive the animals from whence the sounds in the trees issue, they being most effectually hid among the leaves and branches.

Should the curious Ornithologist, or the prying Botanist, emigrate here, they could not fail of deriving ample gratification in their favourite pursuits in this luxurious museum. Birds, flowers, shrubs, and plants; of these many are tinged with hues that must baffle the happiest efforts of the pencil.

FROM THE LETTERS

BEHOLD A FISH, SPANGLED WITH GOLD

"Genius in bondage", was what he called it,
The way they used him, "an ingenious Artist",

To catalogue in pictorial fashion
The flora and fauna of this distant land.

The Australians sat and watched his eyes flit
From cut flower, dead bird or fish

To the white sheet. They watched the action
Of his brush, and saw a Black-browed Thrush stand

As if alive. Did he bear the grudge he claimed?
Was there pretence somewhere in his lack of passion?

When he painted a fish "spangled with gold", "stained
With dyes brilliant as the arch of heaven",

Could he then forget his lowly station?
Or did he coldly copy Nature down

The way he'd copied a guinea note, frown
At his master and garner his rations?

WHAT PICTURE DO THEY CARRY IN THEIR HEADS?

What picture do they carry in their heads
Of where they are? Even back in Scotland

Maps are for landowners, to be spread
On polished tables, as sharp eyes scan

Their inheritance. Educated types
Like Watling carry Scotia's outline too

Though, for most, their world begins to slip
From them when one day's hard walking's through.

But within their daily world, they'll tell you
The name of each hill, field, forest and stream:

The story behind each they also know.
Australia is someone else's dream.

Give them time. Here too they'll name each cove,
Each inlet, each meeting of land and sea;

Soon be able be lead you to the cave
Of welcome shade, beneath the *Hanging Tree*.

WATLING ANTICIPATES BILLIE HOLIDAY

Bats hang from their branches like ripe black fruit.
Strange Fruit. And though that melody can't haunt

His mind, their high keening begins to flit
Through his night, leaving him, come morning, gaunt

And unslept. They can latch onto darkness
Itself. That doesn't augur anything well.

He's been transported to a world of signs:
The sleek skin of a ghost gum with its folds

Of rippled flesh, like the tattered banners
Of the paperbark tree, speaks of Death –

Their leather-leaves cannot deceive him. Nor
Will the White Ibis restore his faith:

A bill like a surgical instrument
On the black knob of its head; just the tool

To ask for, as the patient lies there, spent,
And you probe for the lead ball lodged in his skull.

DROUGHT TURNS HIS THOUGHTS TO HOME

One year without rain. Every day the same
Blue skies like a mockery above him,

Though, inside his head, seasons turn. His crime
Distinguishes him like an extra limb:

He waits for it to wither in the heat.
October now, and the Nith runs by him

Swollen and dark. Rain salts between its pleats.
For some weeks, a dislodged tree's been jammed

At the weir. The water's stripped it back
To a smooth, almost marbled, black. From rimmed

Eyes, darker than even that, the slim sack
Of one cormorant parts its beak and grins

At another. Its wings are spread like Death.
Sometimes, inside his head, is a sermon

That gives no comfort. It says, Save your breath;
Here or there, you've neither friends, lovers, nor kin.

WATLING REACTS FAVOURABLY
TO A FREAK FALL OF SNOW

The first pixel of snow falls on the crest
Of a cockatoo. It's invisible.

More falls and soon there is a second crest.
The cockatoo shakes, blinks a cold black eye.

The crowns of the gum trees begin to fill
With snow. Their arrowed leaves are crisped with frost.

Across the cove, waves stand to attention;
Even the officers blow on their hands.

Watling strides over the small plantation.
What a day to be alive! The raised drills

Ring like metal beneath his feet. Large bats
Bomb softly onto the snow. White pillows

Mark where they lie. And still the snow falls
Over the city's imagined streets.

Even at the suburbs it doesn't stall;
Generations of barbies fizzle out.

A HISTORY LESSON FROM LINGERIE GIRL

Up at Glenroy Hotel, *Lingerie Girl*
Leans on the bar, moves her feet back, becomes

A perfect bracket. Her body is furled
In a scarlet bodice and her bum-buns

Are small and white. When customers applaud
Her gyrations, she kneads flesh in her fists.

Lingerie Girl turns to them with a smile
Sunny as a sandy cove. When she lifts

A leg onto the high table where the men sit,
She reveals a dip at her thigh's top edged

With foaming lace. It's as if a punchline's
Written there. Above their heads, jockeys

Pass over the large screens dressed like parrots.
In the night, Watling hears the women squawk.

Sodom and Gomorrah's no worse than this –
A nation founded on gun, whip and cock.

WATLING PLAYS DOMINOES: A NOCTURNE

There is the shushing of small waves, wind
As it rakes through the frond-like fingers

Of a casuarina. Cries linger
In the air: birds, bats, but also the kind

That come from someone clasping their stomach
In pain, trying to contain what must be said –

That this is another way to be dead;
That each night-sound just increases the ache

For the shadow-world that will always be
More real than this one. And then the other moans

Come. "Turn will you? *Just turn.*" The heart is stone,
The body and only the body sees

What will be done. This bat-world is wrapping
Its wings around itself. Through the darkness

A familiar voice tiredly presses:
"Did ye no hear me? I'm chappin', chappin'."

THOUGHTS TO DEPRESS A MAN OF SENTIMENT

Cheek by jowl, arse to arse – how could Watling
Escape stories of those grim early days?

Blackened bodies, pocked from smallpox, floating,
Their eyes pecked out, in the sparkling bay,

Or lodged like flotsam between the rocks.
Then the other tales of near starvation –

Convicts so weakened they could barely walk
To the whip; gleaners of tiny rations.

Those who've survived still wear a haunted look
In their eyes; their images stalk his dreams.

But now, they whisper that *Boney* might knock
On their door. To Watling, the horizon

Is already like a full sheet of flame:
He imagines great battles beyond it –

In *Australia Incognita*, songlines
Steeped in blood, History enacted in light.

WATLING AND THE PRINCE OF PICKPOCKETS

He met him just the once, George Barrington,
Prince of Pickpockets. He liked the stories

As well as anyone. Covent Garden
And a snuffbox inlaid with diamonds, prised

From Count Orlov. Some whispered George himself
Was of royal descent. Watling thought him

Vain, distrusted someone with such a wealth
Of opinion. Oh, we partners in crime –

True patriots all, for be it understood,
We left our country for our country's good.

Whether or not he authored that couplet,
He authored not much else that bore his name.

Watling, a shadow, sniffs. Let them all sup
Their slops with him; bask in his common fame.

But the Irishman knows what could have been.
That judgement will grace his lunacy.

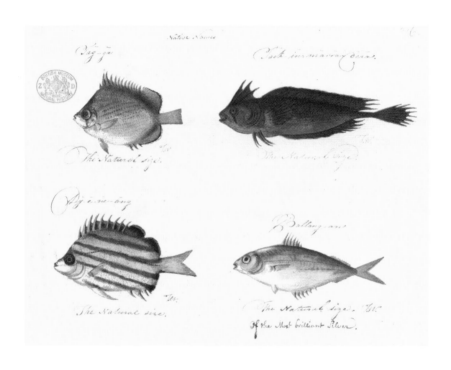

WATLING DREAMS OF THE FISH MARKET

4 a.m. and the Sydney Fish Market
Echoes to the rumble and crack of ice,

The thumping of boxes. Blunt John White,
His knuckles raw, blinks in the glazed blue light.

A Garfish like a silver poker glints
In one fist – a St Valentine's Day gift

For some sucker. Cases of Red Snappers
Burst into flame, cook in his acrid breath.

Oysters, silver in their own jism, sluice
Down his throat; his cocked tongue flicks

Into a mussel's black dish. He cracks
A Swimmer Crab's blue legs – briny juices

Course down his chin. He crunches up shells;
Gnashes and spits through Watling's dream –

Slings him lines of Parrotfish, Yellowtail,
Groper, Grunter, Drummer, Snook, Sweep and Bream.

THE FIRST AND FINAL POEM

Oh, *Home is the first / and final poem.*
Though that line lies so far in the future,

He feels it here, now, "along the margin
Of some nameless stream". His Romantic heart

Can't help but make himself the centre
When he writes – he is *The Man of Feeling*

Without a doubt. The warm night is gentle;
"Coveted solitudes" has the right ring.

He prays for the most loved of aunts; often
"The willing tear" will fall. Is this deceit

Once more, forgery pumping through his veins?
Or greater failure on my part to seek

Him there, pinned in the croaking darkness,
His brush-fingers stiff from his day's labours –

As his aunt sits in her den in Dumfries
And turns to the calumny of *Neighbours*.

LETTERS! LETTERS!

lttrs! lttrs!
lik staring in2 th sun. we walk

arnd lik blind men. i send ths out
lik a messag frm th moon.

r u receivng me
dearst C–

its not th lite
divides us most. its not th lite

its not th sun. neithr nite nor day
wintr nor summr   mnths nor yrs

bt what i no of hungr & pain
th screams of th whippd carried in th wind

& evn if Godwillng somday my ships
in yr port surf poundin the rocks

still i will b in anthr place. this is truly
th botny bay of botny bay

THE PEOPLE ARE in general very straight and slim, but extremely ill featured; and in my opinion the women more so than the men. Irascibility, ferocity, cunning, treachery, revenge, filth, and immodesty, are strikingly their dark characteristics – their virtues are so far from conspicuous, that I have not, as yet, been able to discern them.

One thing I may adduce to their credit, that they are not cannibals. They burn and bury their dead, but from what motive it is hard to conceive; immolation it cannot be; as they have not apparently the smallest idea of a Deity, much less of religion.

FROM THE LETTERS

WATLING AND THE AUSTRALIANS

1. *The Uses of Time*

So they sit and watch him, the Australians
He's so few good words for. For hours they crouch

In silence. What use do they have with hours?
Days? Weeks? They bear the same provision

Of Time; store it in an indolent house.
There, it fuels little to please his eye.

At times, he thinks he's surrounded by shades.
He wonders whether they see what he sees –

The spindle-shaped fish art cannot master
(He hasn't the powders in his palette).

Are they merely mimicking his gesture
Or is there understanding in the click

Of the tongues on the roofs of their palates?
He draws concentration from them now:

Their ancestors at the ancient rock-plates
With their shell-chisels and their furrowed brows.

A Groupe on the North shore, of Port Jackson, New South Wales

2. Night Fires

Though he speaks ill of them, he finds himself
Drawn to the Australians' night fires –

The sharp smell of eucalyptus, the stealth
Of fish oil as it spreads through the flames.

It's for the shapes they make he comes here –
Not to rehearse their strange, vowelly names.

Yet they make space for him. Their children dance
And clack with wood and tongue, while the fish cooks.

Watling looks / draws / looks himself into a trance.
He sees past *puris naturalibis* –

Breasts moulding the humid air; the men's cocks
Limply unguarded. He has painted lists

Of all that moves through this place, but few core
Family scenes. He'll paint them in dark

Greys and blacks, enfolded by rock. More
Ghosts than even prisoners are. Yes, that stark.

3. Baneelon, a Failed Experiment

The marines dressed them, for sport, in paper suits
To mask a nakedness never quite real.

But, for their captive pet – a red jacket
With silver epaulettes. He could toast

The King and had met him too in some cold
Outer Darkness. (Soon, the mad will be cured

By the same shadow play of etiquette
And shame.) Watling passes him in his cups,

A danger to men and women alike,
Scarred where the calls for blood have been answered.

And he judges him a poor counterfeit:
The problem, that singular watermark.

Forgers used a sharp knife for it. They scraped
Into the heart of the paper, gently –

As if lifting the fibres of a leaf.
Sir, send you me please some handkerchiefs.

THE FIRST GULAG

1. Educating the Politicals

The screams are like crystals in the cold air;
Each one of the same kind, yet each unique

In the way it trails or anticipates patterns
Of pain. Some *zek* is getting his Dozen.

After the first strokes, his back is streaked
With blood. The rhymes that follow will tear

The flesh away. "That'll teach the Oirish!"
Some fool shouts. The rest look to their work.

The earth is frozen; it will yield nothing.
The cold-eyed birds and the glassy-eyed fish,

And all the other creatures that lurk
In this place, know it'll soon be over.

There are times Watling must break the ice
To get at his paints. Some time when he does

He'll catch a forgetfulness that covers
This land; its bone-white Siberian cries.

2. Watling Does His Time,
While the Irish Head North

He painted what was placed in front of him.
This is a Bearded Dragon; this a swift.

He tried not to dream. Where would that get you?
The Irish thought to China. They set out –

Their minds alive with thoughts of opium,
Silk, tea, of copper-skinned people with gifts.

They took out a scrap of paper marked *North*. Crows
Found them, hunger found them. It was a rout

Long before they reached the river they thought
Separated the willow-patterned world

From their vale of tears. Survivors wandered
The bush, their lips stained with berries, their flesh

Wasted. Recaptured, they began to plot
Their next escape. The meek would have power,

The tired would rest. There would be no hunger.
Look! Watling says, look at the Frivolous Thrush.

3. Watling Envies the So-called Martyr, Thomas Muir, Transported for Disseminating Paine's Rights of Man.

Thomas Muir, Scottish Martyr; he who stood
Shoulder to shoulder for the *Rights of Man.*

The cameos show him handsome and proud,
Though don't ask Watling. He wasn't a fan

Of the sly Dissident, softly set up
On Hunter's Hill, a farm with a fine view

Of the river. Where was the bitter cup
Watling drank from? No time for Muir to stew –

The *Otter* bore him away. Watling
Painted on. The flora and fauna

Were endless: he'd no time for rebel songs.
Amor fati – we're all nothing but pawns.

Yet, even with half his face shot away,
Covered with a mask specially hand sewn,

Muir filled his lost memoir with tales that say,
"My heart was broken, but I willed it so."

THERE ARE, THANK GOD, no fetters for the soul: collected in herself, she scorns ungenerous treatment, or a prostitution of her perfections; nor will she meanly pluck the laurel from her own brow, to deck that of her unworthy governor. Let it suffice to Britain, that my youthful hopes and reputation are levelled in the dust, and that my old age will be unhoused and indigent; but never let her presume to barter to interested men, the efforts of the artist, or powers of the mind; for these are placed infinitely above her reach.

FROM THE LETTERS

WATLING'S LEGACY – THE FLORA AND FAUNA OF "TERRA NULLIUS"

1. Introducing the Echidna (The Spiny Anteater) and Some Stories Told About It.

How did you do it? Turn the *Mother*
Of All Monsters – as the Greeks once called her –

Into a spiky hot water bottle?
It's said, when spooked, this monster will smother

Herself with earth; that she subsists on ants
And on dew that she licks with a tongue

Red as a whip. What's more, she'll leave her haunt
At the sound of a whistle, her movements

So ungainly capture's foregone. Her flesh,
When fresh, is considered a delicacy.

Looking at your painting again, I see
A heartbeat of socks, a pyjama case –

Whatever, it has none of the life-spark
Of your birds. The truly new is hard to paint.

Echidna, kangaroo. The line is faint.
We hear your stammers, your attempts to speak.

2. Legend

"Plumb-weighted", D.H. Lawrence once called it
And Watling would've said he'd called it right,

Were it not for the elegant pull
In the other direction, the teasing out

Of the torso, the dog-like head stock-still
As the ears scoop sound from the dust-dry air.

Of course Lawrence, sketching his kangaroo
In Taronga Zoo, can't have seen quite how

They absorb the landscape, tracking you
Like boulders from the shade. They're first to know

You're riding into a bushwhacker's trap.
And neither at night does the landscape let up:

It watches, listens, secretes what it sees.
Watling, at the edge of firelight, stares

Back. He wears the night like an iron mask –
Each blue-black rivet is a hidden star.

3. Lorikeets

As if when God's finished creating light
He has some left over he's loath to waste

So he weaves the scraps he has – a few bright
Threads around his feet, on the edge of sight

But dazzling as flower beds in the white
Fields of snow – and from these the lorikeets

Are born. They are concentrations of light –
Light spectra on the wing. Hear them greet

Their own pleasure – chests rose hips in sunlight;
Imagine an autumn hedgerow in flight!

Each day before him the dead are laid out.
He's watched the air spill from their wings – the shout

Of someone's success. As they fall, the bright-
Ness leaves their eyes. He learns when not in flight

They preen each other, for each takes delight
In the other. Lorikeets mate for life.

4. *Watling Paints a Banksia, Or,*
The Dark Side of Enlightenment

Watling has been studying the vulva –
Seedhead of a flowering *Banksia*.

A segment of the ripened bell-shaped fruit's
Been removed, so that the eye is brought

To its hidden centre. Here the winged seeds
Meet like jostling moths or like brittle folds

Of flesh – open but lapping into darkness.
His finger hollows out the seedhead, lets

The seeds helicopter onto his page.
Watling's been studying the women's ways:

How they choose to sit with one foot drawn up
Half-over the crutch. Like a dark comma,

This gives him pause. Men mistake what they see
For what there is. What first appears showy

Is never the whole story. No matter,
They barter for it with bread, blankets, shirts.

5. *The Turcosine Parrot*

He feels the light heft of it in his hand,
His thumb and fingers round its chest, tucked

Beneath its wings. The smooth thumb of its head –
A startling blue – rolls loosely as he takes

Hold of the quill feathers in his left hand
And gently pulls the wing out like a fan.

He watches as each azure blue feather runs
Into the next, the light blessing each one

Till the wingspan sea-shimmers in the air.
How can he stop giving himself to praise?

What Deity made such a Hell peppered
With Beauty? At the edge of their blue haze

The wing feathers are tipped with black. Back home,
The crows hang from posts like upturned crosses.

In the dreich of his mind, he wonders how
To begin counting his gains, his losses.

TWO HANDS, TWO STORIES

In the candlelight he looks at his hands –
Two maps; two different destinations.

Call one hand *Innocence*. Slowly it turns
From darkness into light and he catches

In it something of a human presence
That is shocking and fresh, like the raised bands

Of flesh that decorate their naked chests
Or the cloth-like folds of an old buttock.

Though the left won't knowingly do you harm,
The right has had a different schooling.

Callused where the fingers like a socket
Hold the brush, his lifeline's planted with grains

Of ink down each tiny tributary.
The right has no scruples: what it sees, it paints.

The left closes on itself like a shell:
He doesn't really know it at all.

WATLING'S EVERYWHEN

Years later, up some dark and desperate wynd,
Cancer will lick flesh from him as sun

Had once lifted his skin. He'll taste again
The scorching air of New South Wales – each breath

A fur-ball in his throat. How the women
Palmed their thin skirts down! – as a sudden wind

Whipped round Circular Quay. Close to death
He'll tug at me; something he has to say:

He hopes to have given me the Beauty
And the Horror of what his life has been.

He's wanted to show what cannot be said.
From these threads, let me weave my own stories.

And, as his deranged performance draws near
To its end, he'll tell me its *everywhen*

Was the moment the worn nib of his name
                    Became
The eye he passed through to the pardoned men.

PART THREE:
CALCUTTA

"Daily, Calcutta disintegrates, unwhispering,
into dust, and daily it rises from dust again."

AMIT CHAUDHURI
from *A Strange and Sublime Address*

"Over the ruins
          of hundreds of empires,
The people work."

RABINDRANATH TAGORE
from *Recovery – 10*

THEY ARE A HANDSOME enough people, the women graceful, the men dark-eyed and straight-backed, when not feigning obeisance. But which is the more indolent race – the Whites or the Natives? That I cannot say. Some of the first, it appears, need forty servants for their quotidian ministrations. There is not a garment put there that is not placed there by a native servant. For his part, the native's work hardly justifies the name – one task, that designated to the so-called ab-dar, being simply to move water around during the night to cool the humid air.

It seems, to this observer, that it is only to matters of stupidity and cruelty that they apply ingenuity and energy.

FROM THE LETTERS (UNPUBLISHED)

I

By the time Watling disembarks,
Calcutta's already the hoover-head
                    through which the wealth

Of the continent will pass: bolts of colour
And jolts of taste to enliven the palates of
                        The *Sceptred Race.*

In Calcutta, it's said, money flies through the air.
All you have to do is to catch it. Everyone's at it –

Trading for an estate or for a bowl of rice,
While desperately trying   to cut Death
                            out of the action.

Palace after palace, full-sailed facades,
                              glittering in sunlight:
A fleet to "awe the Indians into submission".

Watling feels, momentarily, a sense of *schadenfreude*
For the agglomeration of makeshift shacks

He's left behind, clinging to the edge
                              of the empty continent.
Here, names are already inhabited by History
            or experience: his landing place –

Golgotha. Crows command the air space.
            They tell him his designation, *Survivor*,

            is far from assured.

II

Hello. How are you? Where you from?
Scotland, ah yes, Scotland.

        Beside the Netherlands, that's Scotland.

Ah yes, it's Noroway in my mind.
So what is bringing you to Calcutta?

Interesting, sir. Do you have football team?
Don't forget, you visit my shop
        before you leave. I do you good deal.

Watling grimaces, gives a curt nod;
Disappears down one of those foetid alleys
        expressly built for the purpose.

But then again, always, the other questions:
The stick-like foot brushing up
                      against him from the ground,

The fingers blindly poking his arm;
The tin plate rattling on the pavement
                      from the cowl-covered shape he passes.

To each question, the same (unhelpful) answer:
"He flourished as a flower in the field.

                      The wind passed over it

And he was gone." Though in these parts, sir,
In one form or another, always
                      you must be returning to the same old shop.

III

Between Black Town and White Town –
Never quite White Town,

        no, never-ever quite White Town –

Watling, in his scratcher, never the master,
                but nor now the slave,
Lies among craftsmen, carpenters, half-castes,

A few sailors who've fled
The unsettled life of the sea; each of them lodged

In a crack between worlds
Where all they can see

        is how much further to fall.

Lies listening, as a pack of dogs,
                              splintered with rage,
Rip the night apart. But, above the dogs'

Murderous howling, above the moans
Of the sick and the lonely; above even
                    the Righteousness he cannot shift –

The torment that these dogs are but the barbs
Of a lifetime's accumulated hurts –

There is the old excitement, born now
                    from more than its own arrogance.
Ask of the Artist what he must do.

                    That he will fulfil.

IV

Such a balmy March day
        on the banks of the Hooghly.
A wheel floats in the blue above the carnival crowd.

Metal hooks are thrust through the willing flesh
Of those who, hoisted, may be birled
           till their flesh is torn,

Their bodies thrown clear. And all the while,
A mendicant's withered arms twine
        over his head, like branches.

        His nails – those of a bird of prey –
Claw at his own wrists, root themselves
          in his scant flesh.

A red hot spike pierces a tongue like butter.
At the back of the crowd, Watling winces

With distaste. The floggings they made him witness:
Penance or punishment aye make a bloodied map
                              of some poor sod's back.

He would rather be spending his freedom with me
Down at Babu Ghat,
                    where bold river sprites leap

Rim upon rim of rotting filth
                    into the grey waters of the Hooghly –
To rise, gleaming, shriven,
                         through hoops of dusty air.

V

Then, like now, away
   from the broad Imperial drags
With their palanquins, rickshaws and carriages

(The boxlike buses, the battered blue trams) –
The huff and puff
   of an almost adolescent impetuosity –

There is, where cradles of light lift the shadows,
A concatenation
   of human activity. On one street corner,

Children so close to the dust, it seems
   their blue-black skin merges with it.
But their eyes are bright as two

     lightly clicking marbles.

Night fires.
      A woman stirring a pot on a trestle table,
Men at cards on cardboard mats;
                  air sweet with spices

And flaming pucks of dung. Watling feels again
                  that tug of the hearth;
The small coals that give life to the heart.

      ~

And now, a man on a bike, knees akimbo –
Two rows of dead white hens

Like a frilled skirt around him.
Poultry lanterns glowing in the smoky air.

VI

Back in New South Wales
      they'd brought his subjects to him
Dead.

His task had lain in making them –
The beautiful birds – seem
            as if alive. He'd become

A *Resurrectionist* of sorts. But here,
His subjects come to him while alive

And his trick is to disguise what he sees
Of what *Life's*
            Inconstant Tide might bring.

The pink-headed duck. Of course,
He couldn't hunt them himself
                    in the jungle north of Calcutta;

He was no one's idea of a sportsman.
But he saw them being brought in – a brace,

Slung, with a tiger, from a pole.
The vibrancy of that pink blush – from the base
                    of their necks to their heads –

Disarmed him. *Opal pink*? Cowrie pink? *Sea pink pink*?
And then, what pose for the bird
                    that would not survive its own beauty?

VII

It's not as if he hasn't looked Despair
                    in the face before:
The slack skin, the lifeless eyes
                    of the homesick

And the hopeless, before their hearts cracked.
But he'd been more accustomed to studying
                    the illegible faces of birds,

Their impenetrable black eyes. He'd painted
                    the parrot with delight,
But not seen the parrot, when alive,
                    delight in its own display.

This had pleased his Scottish heart.
But the likenesses he is painting now? –

In his frock coat when Watling arrives, his skin
Milky blue, in spite of the heat; a kiss curl
                    plastered to his forehead.

So ornate is this desire for a future,
An afflatus of lace
                    bursts from his chest.

Yet Watling sees past the pose,
          its feigned air of worldly purchase.
The eyes try not to give the *Memento Mori* away –

But why does that hand grip the chair like a claw,
While the other is thrust inside the waistcoat,

                    already distrusting the heart?

VIII

The adjutant bird will swallow a dead cat whole,
Make ready work of a rat
        or a bothersome crow.

One once bore a girl away to a rooftop.
Down another's throat, a baby slipped,
        haltingly, into darkness.

(That bird was not without its critics, yet still,
For services to vermin control, it walked free.)

Bored soldiers lob them,
Bones packed with gunpowder, for the pleasure
        of watching them exploding in flight.

Watling's observed the birds walk, stooped
Like old men, hands beneath their coat-tails,

Bald heads nodding; first one way, then the other,
As if observing new arrivals at the Captain's Ball.

Of those lucky enough to land a young officer,
The adjutant, Death, will take his pick,
                    gathering them from child-bed

In the great hammock of its wings.
Before the paint on the keepsake's dry,
                    a fresh prospect mounts the funeral steps.

IX

Now he's got the hang of Karma, Watling thinks
He could well come back

                                as a crow –

Sleek, oily blue, purged of emotion:
"Above the packed and pestilential town,

                               Death looked down."

Indeed, a crow's eyes have their interests.
Each day, he'd watch the city rise from the dust

                          into the giant puzzle of itself;

In the evening's golden light, he'd preen
On a slate-blue obelisk. One that inscribed a life in

                           years   months   days.

But, of all creatures, especially, Dear God,
Not one of those fucking dingo dogs

With mealy tits and hollow hips, kicked
Even from the shadows where it lies.
                              Not one of those

Forced into the humid night
To fight with the pack, though in its heart

It is a loner. Not one of those
Whose dull, lustreless eyes
                    are earthbound, mournful and sensate.

X

What would Watling give to see someone
Commandeer one of the swarms
                of snub-nosed yellow taxis

That nudge, whinge and honk around town?
To see his hero lead them, red flag in hand,
                roaring up Chowringhee,
Scattering
                palanquins, peons, and hurcarrahs;
Making carriages bolt
                and all the dainty parasols

Fly, till they fall gently into the Hooghly,
Like the silken blossoms of the Drooping Asoke;
                of the delicate white

                White Murdha.

I cross Howrah Bridge,
          through the end-of-day heat,
The shoals of traffic; the trains of traders, bent,

Like shell-bearers,
          margined in a darkened miniature.

It's been said, *We are each a story in the making,*
Creating our lives
          through the choices we make.

Watling squats, cradling his chest of lost connections.

"If my life's dream must be told," he begins.
But his tongue, like a fizgig, sticks:
          "Water. Please. More water."

XI

Night. Fever. Visions.
In the river,
            the decomposing, bloated bodies turn.

In the watery shadows, they layer,
                        one on the other;
Glimpses of the secret corners lovers make.

A bull rolls over, its sacred belly split
Into a flagon, fountaining blood. Watling moves

Through the terrors of childhood – Ghouls,
                        Bogles, Brownies and Sprites:
Come, cast these darker mindscapes
            from the waking sight.

Watling thinks, in a moment's stillness,
                               he should pray.
He begins with the comfort of Catechism:

But finds it comforts him not.
He attempts the mighty set pieces.

                           The wind blows through them.

He addresses the great heavenly constellations.
The buttery moon turns from him.

                           It has its own song to sing.

Watling decides his prayer will be Silence.
And he is answered by his own heart's
                               imperfect beating.

Sierra-da

Caib-bow-ah

Bal-bow-ah

PART FOUR:

RETURN

"in immortality now I fix
my anchor for peace and rest"

THE ADVENTURER RETURNS

It's that *Local Hero* moment, the one
Where McIntyre, home again, with Houston

Burning up like an oil refinery
Beyond the glass wall of his window, finds,

In the depths of a pocket, a handful
Of shells. The first rule of the exile's school:

You are where you cannot be. The phone rings
Over the sands. We're left with his longing.

So Watling, though Dumfries isn't quite Houston,
Looks over the few dim lights of the town –

The candles, the dying hearths, the new bridge
Arching darkly over the frozen Nith –

And takes from his coat pocket, between thumb
And forefinger, a few odorless crumbs.

Only *his* memories, unlike a lick
Of these once sharp leaves of eucalypts, stick.

SAMUEL JOHNSON ANTICIPATES WATLING, 1773

On his journey through the Scottish Highlands,
Samuel Johnson had a party trick –

He could imitate that strange new creature,
The kangaroo. Clearing a space, he stood

Erect and put his hands out like feelers.
In those dark houses, they turned up the wicks

To miss nothing. He trailed his own pleasure
As he gathered up the tails of his coat

To become the pouch of the animal.
Then, as the watchers mimicked terror,

Half as devil and half as drunken goat,
He made two vigorous bounds, wall to wall.

With greater acquaintance of the real thing,
Do you, Thomas, do the like on return?

Something in *The Globe* to break up the songs,
To spread a laughter so bitter it burns.

Red breasted (or blue bellied) Parrot, Syn x 212

Lambert Drawing vol 1. pt XI

Red breasted, or Blue bellied Parrot. Latham Syn... 1 p 212

Native name Goevil

This Parrot has a fine white Tongue like the Drawing, No 300,
Psittacus hæmatodes variety, called the blue bellied Parrot; see Latham Syn

THE MAKING OF THE ARTIST WATLING

It took Australia to forge an Artist
Out of you. You needed the light, the silence

That stalked its "luxuriant museum".
You needed White's using of you, his lists

Of flora, fauna; barely named, endless
As Creation. For in the tedium

Something came alive, both in your paint brush
And in yourself. Like the Hakea tree,

Whose nut-like cone feeds on bush fires to seed,
So your talent thrived in heat. You returned,

Bearing the secrets of "Lapis Lazuli,
India Marbling and Tortoiseshell".

On home ground, a proud devilment burned
Quietly in your antipodean eye.

Your work was – you vouched the sharp-eyed would feel –
"Not easily discovered from the real".

WATLING DOES A SELLING JOB

Experts say Watling's *View of Sydney Cove*
Was painted from sketches back in Dumfries –

He had no access to oil paints till then.
So he's salvaged a sketch, its edges creased

And torn. He wants to smooth out all that's rough
And troubling about that desert, within

One stretched canvas, with the gloss of oil paint.
Of all things he wants this painting to be,

The greatest is a *Performance*. He points
To it with his brush. This one finally

Will knock them dead. His ill fame's secured
This evening's patronage. The gentlemen

Warm the claret in their hands. He measures
His success, but more their condescension.

Fuck them! They're nothing but a bunch of Whites.
"Most interesting, Watling. Thank you. Goodnight."

WATLING'S CHILD

1. Rogue and Whore

We have so little, I sit in my attic
Forging you from scraps. No apologies.

One source claims that to a nameless convict
You had a son. None of the cornstalks' cries

Have survived, but of him I'd love to know
For sure. It's said the boy sailed with you:

Meaning she, who wished for a heart of straw,
Committed her son to a better life.

What good could come from "the coupling of rogue
And whore"? you wrote; your "wife" a common thief

Brought so far for stealing a winter cloak.
Irish she was and spoke it too, her English

A foreign language to you both. Your throat
Was dry the night you lay and unstitched

Each other. She turned her face from that shore
And swore, twice love-shorn, she would lose no more.

2. The Living and The Dead

So whatever happened to Watling's child?
In Calcutta, he learned to mix the paints,

To pass his father camel-hair brushes.
Still a miniature himself, a smile – faint

But sure – sustained him in that teeming place;
Till sickness took him and Watling sailed home

Alone. But did his aunt not thrill to see
Him and the wordless child whose heart was stone?

Who wheeped like a peewit in winter fields
And was gone. What happened to Watling's child?

Back there, he'd watched one of *them* dig a grave
For his wife. On her chest he'd placed their child

Curled in bark, then dropped a large stone on both
The living and the dead. Just so you'd drown

A litter you saw no way to support.
Thus, mother and child both became unnamed.

MARKET DAY, DUMFRIES

On summer evenings, after market days,
He liked to stroll the length of the Whitesands –

The strip where the boy racers come to play
Tig, or to idle side by side and bend

Their ears to talk of revs per minute,
Like farmhands swapping notes on their cattle.

All day it has built – the fecund, patient
Reek of shit, breath, blood and hide. In the still

Of the evening, he breathes all of it in.
How those bulls bellowed! Like pumped-up engines.

He saw the leached earth, the cattle dying
In that other place; rationed meat like string,

Rancid from the barrel. This hothouse stench
Along the Sands is a sign of wealth –

Of God's grace for this land. Boy racers crunch
Through their gears; the poor settle in their filth.

WATLING AND THE POLITICAL SPHERE

1. Ornithology

Thomas Watling's beyond caring at whatever's
Happening in Iraq; the Palestinian question

Leaves him cold. At the same time he wonders
What months the desert birds will be nesting

In these lands and how their pinion feathers
Knit across their backs. And names? What names

Do the songbirds have? And do they gather
In flocks or play solitary mating games?

He's no desire to have an interest
Once more imposed on his brush. There are books

Galore with the info: even the internet
Will sort out your Iraqi crows and rooks.

Yet still he thinks there's something to be said
For a ceasefire in which the birds are plucked

From the sky, their names burnished; till his dread
Of the desert – Silence – wakes him up.

2. *Watling Dreams of What is His Due*

Thomas Watling, the First Minister said,
Is one of our greatest without a doubt.

Transported, put upon, underfed,
Yet he became Scotland's own Audubon –

An earnest Australian frontier scout.
He gave us the Banksian Cockatoo,

The Pacific Gull, the Soft-tailed Flycatcher
With its chest of cerulean blue.

We should honour a man of such stature!
At the back of the chamber, Watling sighs.

At last the interviews, the colour features.
He waits, as he always has, for Life's Prize.

But I ask you, the Minister continues,
Wherefore, thereafter, the artistic drought –

The sign painting, the humdrum, then the news
Of the forgery for which he still must account?

A STRIKING SIMILARITY BETWEEN
THE LAST LETTERS OF BURNS (1796)
AND WATLING (1814)

"Forgive, forgive me!" he wrote at the end
Of his days, terrified, for all his songs,

That jail beckoned for the want of five pounds.
He penned *Crystal Devon, winding Devon*

While a fine "wretch of a haberdasher"
Jangled his failing nerves. Two weeks later

He was dead. What had been done to foster
The genius of this unique debtor? –

The question finally asked when he'd gone.
They were still talking up the funeral

When Watling returned. He heard them all fawn
Over his grave. It made his flesh crawl.

On the back of one priceless guinea note,
Each might have, though only one of them wrote:

Wae worth thy pow'r thou cursed leaf!
Fell source of all my woe and grief!

AFTER MANY YEARS OF SILENCE,
A LAST REQUEST

The last act, we believe, comes in London.
Helpless, he turns to Admiral Hunter

For "pecuniary relief". His pen
Echoes in the hollow room. The former

Governor – "worthy Sir" – must have been kind
To him in the past. Thus, a "tear steals down

[His] pallid countenance," writing these lines.
Thomas Watling, tell, is this your last throw

Of a loaded dice? As an honest man
At last, do you see the good Governor

Where first you saw him, under the hot sun
Of the distant colony? Glimmerings

Of feathers, scales, petals in pen and paint:
Were they enough to extend your account?

You write of a cancer in your "left breast".
No evidence Hunter dealt with your request.

POSTSCRIPT

KEEN TO HOLD A GUINEA NOTE IN MY HAND, I CONTACT HBOS MUSEUM ON THE MOUND IN EDINBURGH

"Hi, Sian, thanks for the material you sent.
Though none of the guinea notes you have

Are forgeries, if I may, I still want
To hold, albeit in its acetate,

One squat milky note (those intricate waves
Of black script) to the lucid East coast light.

I'll find the mark that guarantees its worth.
Through this porthole, I'll glimpse the Forth."

                 ★

"Hi, Tom, I'm glad you enjoyed your visit.
I'm sure you'll be interested to know

Our bank notes have been seen by an expert.
True guinea notes have thicker paper,

Their detail is much clearer and sharper.
Turns out *all* our guinea notes are forged." So,

This is a good time to believe in ghosts,
To hear, through the *e* universe, laughter.

A WILD ADVENTURE:
NOTES

PRELUDE: A WORLD OF LIGHT
Copious notes were taken by the early naturalists, regarding the accuracy of colourings and shape, but none regarding sound. Similarly, it took many years before artists realised that to depict the Australian landscape the prime element was not form but light.

PART ONE: ARREST

THE BANK OF SCOTLAND ADVISES ITS DUMFRIES AGENT DAVID STAIG,
20 SEPT 1788
It was the same determined David Staig who pursued Watling for his second (unproven) forgery in 1806. One of the ways of authenticating bank notes was to match them against the individual cuts of their stubs.

WATLING'S DIRGE: SCOTIA FAREWELL
This "dirge" is based on broadsheet publications of the time which stressed contrition and the possibility of reform. Not, it would turn out, Watling's style!

PART TWO: TRANSPORTATION

ON BOARD SHIP, BOUND FOR THE COLONY
"Malt juice and pickled cabbage put Europeans in Australia as microchip circuitry put Americans on the moon." Robert Hughes, *The Fatal Shore.*

THE AFTERLIFE OF NAMES
The Australians fought ritual battles over voicing the name of a dead man. The uttered name could summon havoc from the spiritual realm into the physical earth. After death, the deceased became "a nameless one".

WATLING PLAYS DOMINOES: A NOCTURNE
I am indebted to *Gulag, A History* by Ann Applebaum (2003) for some of the details in this poem (concerning extremes of homesickness and violence) and in the sequence entitled *The First Gulag.*

WATLING AND THE PRINCE OF PICKPOCKETS
George Barrington (1755-1804) was Sydney's first celebrity criminal. The couplet concerning "True patriots" was written by Henry Carter in 1801, but included in a work ascribed to Barrington.

THE FIRST AND FINAL POEM
The Man of Feeling is the title of a novel (1771) by Henry Mackenzie. It created a new kind of hero, the sensitive man, as opposed to the Man of Reason.

LETTERS! LETTERS!
In his account of the early years of the settlement (1790), Watkin Tench writes, "Letters! Letters! was the cry. They were produced and torn open in trembling agitation."
"Dearest C" is addressed on occasion in the *Letters.* Nothing is known about her.

WATLING AND THE AUSTRALIANS

2. Night Fires
The colonisers brought death. "Sydney" was invaded in 1788. In one migration the number of Europeans equalled about half the original population. The sudden influx of people was catastrophic. Within a year the Australians were dying of smallpox. One band that was 50 in 1788 numbered 3 in 1790. 70% of the mammals died.
To the Australians, fire was shelter. As Robert Hughes writes in *The Fatal Shore* (1986), "Hearth was of far greater significance than home."

3. Baneelon, a Failed Experiment
Baneelon (or Bennelong) was captured on the orders of Governor Phillip. He was taken to England in 1793, where he was described by the press as "the Cannibal King". He returned to Sydney in 1795. He found no acceptance among his own people or among his English "benefactors". He died in 1813. *The Sydney Gazette* commented,

"Of this veteran champion of the native tribe little favourable can be said. His voyage to and benevolent treatment in Britain produced no change whatever in his manners and inclinations, which were naturally barbarous and ferocious."

The closing line of the poem is from a letter, written by Baneelon in 1796, to his English friend Mr Phillips, Lord Sydney's steward. It is his only surviving writing.

THE FIRST GULAG

1. Educating the Politicals
Zek was what a prisoner was known as in the Soviet gulag.
A Botany Bay "Dozen" was twenty-five lashes.

2. Watling Does His Time, While the Irish Head North
Alexander Majoribanks, in *Travels in New South Wales* (1847) states that "A man is banished from Scotland for a great crime, from England for a small one, and from Ireland, morally speaking, for no crime at all." The Irish were constantly and hopelessly trying to escape. They thought if they headed north they'd end up in China. Robert Hughes uses this to show how uneducated they were. But an Australian of Irish descent in Sydney pointed out to me the logic of their decision – often the ships that brought convicts went on to China to load up with tea and so to turn a profit. This sequence is based on the observation by Robert Hughes that the colony anticipates the "vaster, more efficient techniques of class destruction that would be perfected a century later in Russia." It was said you could pass fifty skeletons in a day's walking from the penal colony.

1. Watling Envies the So-called Martyr, Thomas Muir, Transported for Disseminating Paine's 'Rights of Man'.
Thomas Muir was transported to the colony in 1794 and was rescued after two years.

WATLING'S LEGACY – THE FLORA AND FAUNA OF "TERRA NULLIUS"

2. Legend
This poem borrows from *Kangaroo* by D.H. Lawrence and from imagery in Sydney Nolan's *Ned Kelly* paintings.

4. Watling Paints a Banksia, Or, The Dark Side of Enlightenment
"There was a strong Scottish Enlightenment tradition of the use of illustration, both in teaching and in publication." *Robert Wight and the Illustration of Indian Botany* by Henry Noltie (2006). John Hope, Professor of Botany at Edinburgh University (1791-86), was a key figure in this area of study.

5. The Turcosine Parrot
"His water colour drawings of natural history subjects – particularly of birds – combine artistic sensitivity with scientific accuracy to a rare and remarkable degree." *Early Artists of Australia* by Rex and Thea Rienits (1963).

WATLING'S EVERYWHEN
Everywhen is an Australian-aboriginal concept, denoting an experience one has repeatedly; something that it can be a curse to remember. "Deranged performance" is a phrase from his own *Letters from an Exile in Botany Bay to his Aunt in Dumfries.*

PART THREE: CALCUTTA

The quotation by Rabindranath Tagore is from *Recovery – 10* (*Selected Poems*, translated by William Radice, 1985)

I. It was the Governor-General of India, the Marquis of Wellesley who, in the building of Government House (1799-1803), said, "We must awe the Indians into submission".
   "Survivor" was an informal designation in Calcutta. For those who survived the passage from England (whose deaths were calculated in "Waterloos") and their first monsoon season, there was a "Survivors' Party".
II. "He flourished as a flower ... " is copied from a gravestone in Park Street Cemetery, Kolkata.
IV. The description of The Churuk Pooja is taken from the *Journals of Fanny Parkes* (1822-1846).

VI. The last pink-headed duck died at Foxwarren Park in Surrey in 1936.

VIII. The capabilities of the adjutant bird are taken from *Calcutta – Strange Memoirs, Foreign Perceptions* by T.R. Barrett (2004)

IX. "Above the packed and pestilential town … " is from *Tale of Two Cities* by Rudyard Kipling. The poem concerns his experience of Calcutta in the latter part of the nineteenth century.

X. A "palanquin" is a sedan chair, a "peon" a footman and a "hurcarrah" a messenger.

"*We are each a story in the making …* " These lines are from a discussion of Sartre in *On Stories* (2002) by Richard Kearney.

"If my life-dream must be told," is the opening of Samuel Palmer's *Autobiographical Letter to F.G. Stephens*, 1 November 1871.

PART FOUR: RETURN

THE MAKING OF THE ARTIST WATLING
The quotations here are from Watling's advertisement for art tuition in Dumfries. I have recently been visited by brothers Gary and Trevor Watling, who believe Thomas to be their great great great grandfather. They can trace their own line to a Thomas Watling, who they think to be Thomas's son, a coach painter in Gloucester. But they cannot find the binding proof.

SAMUEL JOHNSON ANTICIPATES WATLING, 1773
Incident reported in *Journal of a Tour to the Hebrides* by James Boswell (1785).

WATLING'S CHILD
Children born to convicts were known as "cornstalks" or "currency children". I have recently been visited by brothers Gary and Trevor Watling, who believe Thomas to be their great great great grandfather. They can trace their own line to a Thomas Watling, who they think to be Thomas's son, a coach painter in Gloucester. But they cannot find the binding proof.

MARKET DAY, DUMFRIES

The Whitesands (the Sands) is that area by the River Nith in Dumfries that was used for markets.

WATLING AND THE POLITICAL SPHERE

1. Ornithology

Bird watching continued throughout the Iraqi conflict.

2. Watling Dreams of What is His Due

For all Watling's pride, it is more apt that Alexander Wilson (b. Paisley 1766, d. Philadelphia 1813) would be described as 'Scotland's Audubon'. Sometimes referred to as the 'Father of American Ornithology', Wilson was born almost twenty years before Audubon.

A STRIKING SIMILARITY BETWEEN THE LAST LETTERS OF BURNS (1796) AND WATLING (1814)

Burns was obsessed with a fear of poverty. A solicitor had sent him a letter for non-payment of a tailor's account for his Volunteer's uniform, stoking his terror of dying in a debtor's prison.

As for Watling, a friend, Richard Mearns, has alerted me to the fact that there is, in the London Metropolitan Archives of Wandsworth, Battersea St Mary, registration of the burial of a Thomas Watling on July 14th, aged 74 years. Richard writes, 'If 14 July 1836 is the correct date of burial and 74 is the correct age, it ties in well with his birth of 1762. It doesn't fit in very well with Watling's claim that he had a cancerous chest in 1814.' There are no further details given, no names of parents, spouse or occupation; nothing to suggest this might be the Watling with whom I am concerned. In any case, surely Watling would never tell such an untruth?

NOTE: All unattributed quotations are from the *Letters from an Exile at Botany Bay* by Thomas Watling, apart from *LETTER V*, which is my own forgery, and the quotations from Watling's letter to Admiral Hunter in *AFTER MANY YEARS OF SILENCE*.

A WILD ADVENTURE:

ACKNOWLEDGEMENTS

I am indebted to a number of books for information and context regarding Thomas Watling. I would like to mention here, *The Fatal Shore* by Robert Hughes (1986), *The Commonwealth of Thieves* by Thomas Keneally (2005) and *Dancing with Strangers* by Inga Clendinnen (2003). I have followed two decisions by Clendinnen. The first is to call "the people the British found living around what was to become Sydney Harbour" *Australians* and the second to use the name, *Beneelon*, rather than the more common *Beneelong*. Clendinnen gives compelling reasons for both decisions. There are many short accounts of Watling's time in Australia in books about early Australian artists, but the only extended biographical essay on him remains that by Hugh S. Gladstone, *Thomas Watling, Limner of Dumfries* (1938). For an introduction to his work and that of early colonial artists, *The Art of the First Fleet: Images of Nature* by Lisa Di Tommaso cannot be bettered; and for the story of natural science and imperialism, *Sex, Botany and Empire* by Patricia Fara is an engrossing read.

Calcutta, The City Revealed by Geoffrey Moorhouse (1971) and *Calcutta* by T. R. Barrett (2004) were among the most useful, for my purposes, of the books I read on Calcutta/Kolkata. However, the books were most useful to me as preparation for the encounters I had and the help I received from people I met in Sydney and in Kolkata; and for the conversations I had in Scotland about Thomas Watling and the worlds he [might have] experienced.

I would like particularly to mention, in Sydney, Malcolm, Wendy and Virginia Broun and the members of Sydney's Scottish History

Society; in Kolkata, for advice before I departed, Bashabi Fraser and Rajorshi Chakraborti; and in the city itself, Anjana Basu, Basant Rungta and the Srijanites literary group.

I am gratel to Professor Ted Cowan for a rich discussion about Watling and mapping and much else and to Dr Stuart Hanscomb for a discussion about existentialism and narrative. I would like to thank him for recommending to me *On Stories* (2002) by Richard Kearney. Sian Yates, Senior Archivist at the Museum on the Mound, inducted me into the mysteries of forgery.

I am grateful to the Scottish Arts Council / Creative Scotland for two Writers Development Grants that allowed me to visit Sydney (2007) and Kolkata (2010) to research this work. Its literature department, under the late Dr Gavin Wallace, showed interest and support throughout.

I am indebted to Bashabi Fraser for her reading of the manuscript, particularly the Calcutta section, and also to Emily Ballou for her reading of the Australian section and for suggesting lacunae in the sequence that I might explore. I always felt that design would be a crucial element in creating the 'world' of this book. For her patience and for her sensitive professional skill I am indebted to Teresa Monachino. And for the cover, my thanks to Jim Hutcheson. My interest in Thomas Watling was sparked by an exhibition, *Thomas Watling – Dumfries Convict Artist*, at Dumfries Museum in 1988. In one way or another, he has been with me ever since. It is therefore a particular pleasure – for which I thank Neville Moir, director of publishing at Polygon – to see *A Wild Adventure* published in 2014, in what is generally accepted as the 200th anniversary of his death.

SACRED TO THE MEMORY OF

THOMAS
WATLING ESQ.

LIMNER OF DUMFRIES
WHO THOUGH DEAD
STILL LIVETH

*He lived disrespected
And he died unlamented*